The Ten-Second Rule in Car Sales

Why First Impressions Determine Whether Customers Stay or Leave

Bruce Huddleston

Bedrock Heritage Publishing

Published by Bedrock Heritage Publishing

A Division of Life Guidance Consulting LLC

Tyler, Texas

www.bedrockheritagepublishing.com

ISBN: 978-1-972179-14-7 (Paperback)

ISBN: 978-1-972179-67-3 (EPUB)

Manufactured in the United States of America

DISCLAIMER

This book is based on the author's personal and professional experiences, observations, and opinions, accumulated over a 35-year career in the automotive industry. It is intended for educational and informational purposes only.

The stories and anecdotes contained in this book are drawn from real-world situations encountered throughout the author's career. However, names, identifying details, specific circumstances, employer names, dealership names, and individual characteristics have been changed, omitted, combined, or fictionalized to protect the privacy of the individuals involved. Any resemblance to specific living persons, current or former employers, or existing businesses is coincidental and unintentional.

No individual, dealership, organization, or employer referenced or implied in the stories within this book has reviewed, approved, or endorsed the content herein. The recollections and characterizations presented are solely the author's own perspective and memory of events and do not constitute a factual record, legal testimony, or statement of fact regarding any identifiable person or entity.

The sales strategies, techniques, and professional advice presented in this book reflect the author's personal approach and experience. Individual results will vary based on experience, effort, market conditions, dealership policies, and other factors beyond the author's control. Nothing in this book constitutes a guarantee of income, employment, or professional outcome.

*For the salesperson on the lot right now, walking out
toward a customer for the first time today.
Ten seconds. Make them count.*

FREE BONUS

Your Complete Digital Script Library

Get the Car Sales Survival Quick-Reference Card — a free companion to this book that
puts the key rules and techniques on one page you can keep at your desk.

Visit:

www.carsalessurvivalseries.com/scripts

Enter your email to claim your free reader bonus.
Print it. Keep it. Use it.

Contents

INTRODUCTION

Ten Seconds Is All You Get

Here is something most salespeople never get told straight.

The customer has already decided what kind of experience this is going to be, sometimes before you finish your first sentence, and sometimes before you even take the first step toward them.

Not consciously. They are not standing on the lot running a checklist in their head. But their nervous system is. Their gut is. The same part of the brain that decided in half a second whether the stranger walking toward them at the gas station last week was safe or sketchy is now deciding the same thing about you.

Ten seconds. That is the window. After that, every word you say has to fight uphill against the impression that is already locked in.

I have watched this play out for thirty-five years. New-car franchises, used-car lots, finance offices, buy-here, pay-here — the location does not matter. The math is the same. The salesperson who reads right in the first ten seconds gets a conversation. The one who does not gets "I'm just looking," and a customer who is already counting the steps back to their car.

Most of what's taught about car sales skips straight to scripts and word tracks. What to say at the meet-and-greet. How to handle objections. What to ask on the walk-around. All of that matters. But all of it lives on top of something more basic. Something that happens before any of it gets a chance to operate.

That something is the ten-second rule.

This is not motivational fluff. It is not a gimmick. There is a name for it in the research world — thin-slicing —, and there are entire studies on how accurately people read each other in the first few seconds of contact. The short version: very accurately. The customer reads you quickly and well. And what they read is not what you said. It is what you carried in with you.

Book 5 of this series covered the approach — the physical walk across the lot, the distance, the opening line. Mechanics. This book goes underneath the mechanics. It is about presence. It is about what is leaking out of you before you open your mouth. It is about the totality of what a customer is registering while you are still ten paces away.

Most of what kills deals in those ten seconds is invisible to the salesperson. He thinks he made a clean approach. He thinks the customer is just being difficult. He has no idea his face said something his words did not, or that his energy walked across the lot before his feet did, or that the customer made up her mind about him while he was still adjusting his name tag.

That is what we are going to fix.

Each chapter in this book breaks down one piece of the ten-second window. What customers register. What they see. What they feel. What you can control. What you cannot fake. And what to do when the first ten seconds go sideways.

Every chapter ends with The Rule—one line. The thing to remember from that chapter is when nothing else sticks. The Rules are the spine of this book. Read them, write them down, put them on a sticky note on your dashboard, do whatever you have to do to keep them in front of you when you walk out onto that lot.

Real stories from the floor show up throughout the book. Things I watched happen. Things I did wrong before I knew better. Things I did right when the pressure was on. None of it was invented. All of it earned.

Here is the deal. By the time you finish this book, you will look at the opening seconds of every customer interaction differently. You are going to notice things you used to miss. You are going to walk out onto the lot tomorrow with a sharper read on what the customer is doing — and a sharper read on what you are doing.

Ten seconds is all you get.

Let's make them count.

"The Rule: The customer has already started forming an impression before you open your mouth. Your job is to make sure that impression works in your favor, not against you."

Chapter I

What the Ten-Second Rule Actually Is

LET ME GET THE soft version out of the way first.

The pop-psychology version of the ten-second rule sounds like a Pinterest quote. Smile. Make eye contact. Be confident. The customer decides about you in ten seconds, so make them count. True enough as far as it goes, but it is the surface. It does not tell you what is actually happening, and if you do not know what is happening, you cannot control it.

Here is the real version.

When a customer first sees you — walking across the lot, standing in the showroom, picking up the phone — their brain runs an automatic assessment. It is not deliberate. It is not optional. It is the same hardwired process that has been running in human beings for hundreds of thousands of years, and it runs whether the person knows it is running or not.

Researchers call it thin-slicing. The brain takes a very small slice of information — a few seconds, a few visual cues, a tone of voice — and produces a fast, complete judgment. Safe or not safe. Trustworthy or not. Worth my time or not. The judgment feels like a feeling, not a thought, which is part of what makes it powerful. The customer is not thinking about you. They are feeling something about you, and that feeling becomes the lens through which everything that happens next is seen.

In the research, thin-slice judgments turn out to be surprisingly accurate. People watching a few seconds of a teacher's lecture rate that teacher about the same as students who sat in the class for a full semester. People shown a silent two-second clip of a doctor talking to a patient can predict whether that doctor has been sued for malpractice. The brain is fast at this and good at it.

Which means the customer walking onto your lot is not making a random snap judgment. They are making a fast and reasonably accurate one. The question is what they are reading.

What Thin-Slicing Reads in a Car Sales Context

In ten seconds, here is what the customer's brain has already taken in:

How do you look? Not how expensive your clothes are. Whether you look put together or as if you slept in your shirt. Whether you look like a professional or like someone who got dragged into filling a shift.

How you move. Walking pace. Posture. Whether you look comfortable in your own body or like you are performing as a salesperson.

Where your eyes are. On them. On your phone. On the building. Scanning the lot for the next opportunity while you are still walking toward this one.

Your face. Specifically, your default face — what your face does when you are not consciously running an expression. We will get into this in detail later. It matters more than you think.

Your energy. The hardest one to describe and the most important. Whether you carry calm or carry tension. Whether you seem present or distracted. Whether you seem glad to be there or are grinding through a shift.

All of that gets read in a window measured in seconds. By the time you say your first sentence, the customer has already decided whether they want to be in a conversation with you or whether they are looking for a polite way out.

Why It Hits Harder in Car Sales

Thin-slicing happens everywhere. The customer running it on you is the same customer who runs it on the cashier at the grocery store, the waiter at the restaurant, and the stranger who sat down next to them on a plane. So why does it matter so much more on a car lot?

Because the customer arrived defensively.

Almost nobody walks onto a car lot relaxed. They have heard stories. They have a brother-in-law who got taken for a ride. They have read articles about negotiating tactics and high-pressure closers. They are bracing for a fight before they ever see you. The defensive mindset is already in place. Their guard is up. Their nervous system is scanning for threats.

So the thin slice they take of you is not neutral. They are not asking "who is this person?" They are asking, "Is this going to be as bad as I expected?" The first ten seconds either confirm their fears or start to dissolve them. There is no middle ground. The customer who arrived defensive is going to leave the first ten seconds either more defensive or less defensive. You do not get to leave them where they were.

That is what makes the ten-second rule different in car sales. In a restaurant, a bad first impression with the waiter means a less pleasant meal. On a car lot, a bad first impression with the salesperson means the customer is already mentally rehearsing how to leave. You are not starting from neutral. You are starting from a deficit, and the first 10 seconds decide whether it grows or shrinks.

The good news — and there is good news — is that the same thing works in reverse. A customer who arrives defensive and gets a clean, calm, professional first ten seconds is a customer whose guard drops faster than they expected. The relief is real. They came in ready for a fight and got a person instead. That is a moment you can turn into a sale.

It Is Not About Performance

Here is what trips up most salespeople when they first hear about all this.

They think the ten-second rule is about performing. Smile bigger. Stand straighter. Be more confident, as if the answer is to crank up the act.

It is not. In fact, that is one of the surest ways to fail the ten-second test.

The customer's brain is doing fast pattern matching, and the pattern it is matching against includes every fake interaction it has ever had. Performed friendliness reads as performed friendliness. A forced smile reads as a forced smile. The customer cannot always articulate what is off, but the thin-slice picks it up instantly. Something feels wrong. The guard goes up, not down.

The ten-second rule is not about putting on a better mask. It is about what you actually are when the customer first sees you. Calm or tense. Present or distracted. Glad to be there or grinding it out. None of those are performances. They are conditions. And conditions leak.

Which means most of the work of mastering the ten-second rule does not happen in the ten seconds. It happens before. In how you show up that day. In what you carry with you when you walk out onto the lot. Whether you took care of the things that would otherwise be leaking out of you in front of the customer.

That is what the rest of this book is about.

"The Rule: Customers form a complete, lasting impression of you in the first ten seconds — not because they choose to, but because their brain is built to. Your job is to know what they are reading and make sure it lands in your favor."

CHAPTER 2

WHAT CUSTOMERS REGISTER BEFORE YOU SPEAK

S TAND AT THE EDGE of any car lot for an hour and watch what customers actually do.

They pull in. They sit in the car for a minute. Sometimes two. They look around. They scan the lot—not the inventory, but the people. They notice who is standing where. They notice whether anyone has seen them yet. They watch the salesperson who steps out the front door long before that salesperson is anywhere near them.

By the time you reach them, you have already been watched for thirty seconds, maybe a minute. The ten seconds we keep talking about are not the ten seconds after you say hello. The ten seconds started when you became visible to them — and the inventory of signals they took in during that window is bigger than you think.

The Inventory

Here is what the customer registers before a word is exchanged. Not in any particular order, because their brain does not sort it in order — it takes it all in at once and produces a single impression.

How did you come out of the building? Did you stride out with purpose? Wander out? Get pushed out by a manager? The body language of someone who chose to come help versus someone who got assigned to come help is completely different, and customers read the difference instantly.

What were you doing before you saw them? If they pulled in and you were laughing with another salesperson, they saw that. If you were leaning on a car, checking your phone, they saw that. If you were standing inside the front door, watching the lot like you were glad to be at work, they saw that too. None of it is invisible. The glass is clear in both directions.

Whether anyone else noticed them first, if you are the second or third person to look at them and not move, the read is already negative by the time you do move. They are not thinking, "thank God someone finally came out." They are thinking, "This is the kind of place where customers wait."

Your pace. We will devote an entire section of this book to pace. A sprint reads as desperate. A slow drag reads as bored. The middle — a calm, deliberate walk — reads as professional. Pace is one of the loudest signals you send, and most salespeople have no idea what their default pace looks like to a stranger.

Your hands. What are they doing? Stuffed in pockets? Crossed? Holding a clipboard like a shield? Hanging naturally? Customers do not consciously evaluate this, but they pick it up. Hands tell a story about whether you are at ease or guarded.

Your face on approach. Not the face you put on when you arrive at the conversation. The face you wear when you are still ten paces out and do not yet know they are looking at you. That face is the real one, and that face is the one they are reading.

Your eyes. Where are they going? On the customer? On the car they are standing next to? On your phone? Scanning the lot for the next person who might be a better lead? Eye behavior on the approach gives away more than almost anything else.

What All of That Adds Up To

Add it all together, and the customer has formed an answer to one question before you ever speak.

Is this someone who is going to help me, or someone I need to defend myself against?

That is the question that runs in the customer's head. Not whether you know the inventory. Not whether you have a good price. Not whether your dealership has a good reputation. Those come later, if they come at all. The first question is the safety question, and they answer it from the signals listed above. They answer it in seconds. And they answer it before you have said hello.

If the answer comes out as "this person is going to help me," the conversation that follows is different. The customer is open. They will tell you what they came in for. They will let you guide the next steps. They will give you the time and information you need to sell them a car.

If the answer comes out as "this person is going to work me," the conversation that follows is defensive. The customer is closed. They say they are just looking. They give you nothing. They count the minutes until they can politely exit. You may still get a deal out of them — occasionally, a customer is so set on a vehicle that they buy despite the salesperson — but you are working against the impression you made before you opened your mouth. Most of the time, the impression wins.

It Starts Before You

One more thing to understand before we move on.

The customer's impression-forming does not start when you become visible. It started when they pulled into the lot. The condition of the building. Whether the showroom looks organized. Whether the cars are clean. Whether other salespeople inside are looking up or scrolling on their phones. Whether the receptionist made eye contact. All of that has already shaped the customer's impression before you walk out the door.

Some of that you cannot control. The condition of the building is not your job. The other salespeople's behavior is not your job. But all of it shapes the deficit or surplus you start with when you walk out to meet the customer.

If the showroom looked sharp and the energy felt right, the customer is already a little more open by the time you arrive. You are starting closer to neutral. If the showroom looks tired and the energy feels off, you are starting in a hole, and your first 10 seconds have to do more work just to dig out of it.

Either way, the inventory of signals is happening before you speak. Knowing what is on that list — and knowing which items you can actually control — is the foundation of working the ten-second rule in your favor.

Here is a story about what happens when the entire team gets this wrong.

FROM THE FLOOR

I walked into a well-known furniture store one afternoon looking for a recliner. Had a specific one in mind. Knew what I wanted to spend. Ready to buy. Three salespeople were sitting on a showroom couch. I could hear them — in earshot, not trying to be quiet — debating whose turn it was to help me. Like I was an interruption to whatever they were doing.

The one who drew the short straw walked over. No greeting. No name. No smile. Just: "What are you here to buy today?"

I said: "Nothing. I'm just looking. I'll let you know if I need help."

And I meant it. They'd lost me in the first five seconds. I didn't buy a thing there. Went somewhere else and bought the same recliner the same afternoon.

The irony is, I walked in ready to spend money. All they had to do was make me feel like a person, not a chore. Instead, they spent more energy arguing over whose turn it was than they spent on the customer standing in front of them. That's not a sales problem. That's a culture problem. And it starts—and ends—with how a team treats the greeting.

Everything that mattered in that store happened before the salesperson opened his mouth. The argument I overheard. The body language of three people on a couch. The fact that helping me was a chore was being passed around. All of that registered. By the time he walked over, the deal was already gone. His first sentence just confirmed what I had already decided.

That is the ten-second rule working against the seller. And the painful part — the part that still bothers me — is that any one of them could have flipped it. Stood up, walked over with a smile, and said something like "Welcome in, take your time, I'm here when you're ready." Done. Sale recovered. The defensive read is undone in eight words. They did not do it because they did not know they were already in the ten-second window. They thought it started when they walked over. It started when I walked in.

That is the lesson of this chapter. The ten-second window opens earlier than you think. By the time you are close enough to greet a customer, they have already decided most of what they need to decide. Your job is to know that, and to make sure the signals you were sending before you opened your mouth told the right story.

"The Rule: The customer's impression of you started forming before you said a word — and before you knew they were watching. Manage the signals you send when no one is looking, because someone always is."

Chapter 3

Appearance: The Signal You Send Before You Move

I AM GOING TO be blunt about this chapter because it needs to be blunt.

How you look matters. Not because the world is shallow. Because the customer's brain is doing exactly what we talked about in Chapter 1 — running a fast pattern match — and one of the loudest inputs to that pattern match is the visible condition of the person in front of them. Before you take a step. Before you say a word. Just standing there. Your appearance is already talking.

And if you show up sloppy, what your appearance is telling the customer is something you do not want said about you.

This Is Not About Looking Rich

Let me head this off at the start. I am not telling you to wear expensive clothes. I am not telling you to buy a watch you cannot afford or upgrade your shoes to something you will be paying off in installments. Plenty of the best salespeople I ever worked with wore the same three shirts on rotation. Their clothes were not the point.

Their clothes were clean. They were pressed. They fit. The salesperson wearing them looked like someone who had taken the job seriously enough to look presentable for it. That is the standard. Not luxury. Care.

The customer is not reading your clothes for price. They are reading them for one signal: does this person look like they take this job seriously, or does this person look like they could not be bothered?

That is the read. Everything else is noise.

What Sloppy Communicates

Here is what a sloppy appearance actually tells the customer, whether you intend it to or not.

It tells them you did not prepare. If you couldn't be bothered to iron your shirt or comb your hair, what else wouldn't you bother with? The customer extrapolates. They do not consciously think, "his shirt is wrinkled, therefore his paperwork will be sloppy." But the impression registers, and the impression is exactly that. Sloppy in one place reads as sloppy across the board.

It tells them you do not respect the room. Customers are dressed for the situation. Some of them dressed up because they think buying a car is an occasion. Some of them rolled in straight from work. Either way, they chose how to present themselves for the interaction. If you look like you did not choose at all — like you wore whatever was on the chair when you woke up — it tells them you do not consider this interaction worth choosing for.

It tells them you do not see them. Appearance is a quiet form of respect. Showing up presentable says, "I knew you were coming. I prepared." Showing up sloppy says, "I did not think about this at all." Most customers cannot articulate that, but they feel it, and they feel it instantly.

It tells them about the dealership. Right or wrong, fair or unfair, you are a representative of the place the moment you walk out the door. A scruffy salesperson on a clean lot creates cognitive dissonance — the customer feels something is off, but doesn't know what. A scruffy salesperson on an already-tired lot just confirms what they feared when they pulled in.

None of that is in your words. None of it is in your sales technique. All of it is in what you looked like when you walked out the door.

The Standard

So what is the standard? I will keep it simple. Here is what showing up looking like a professional means, in plain language.

Clean clothes. Not yesterday's shirt. Not a shirt with a stain you decided you could get away with. Clean. If the day before was muddy or sweaty, the shirt does not get a second shift.

Pressed. Not perfect. Not military creased. But pulled out of the dryer at the right time, hung up, or run through an iron if needed. Wrinkles tell the customer you grabbed it off the floor.

Fits. Too big looks like you borrowed it. Too tight, looks like you forgot you bought it three sizes ago. Clothes that fit communicate that you know what you are doing when you get dressed.

Shoes that are not destroyed. Nobody is asking for new shoes every season. But scuffed, cracked, broken-down shoes show up in the customer's eye whether you want them to or not. Wipe them down. Replace them when they are done.

Hair under control. Combed and trimmed when needed. Facial hair is either kept clean or shaved. Nothing about your head should look like you forgot to deal with it.

Hands clean. People look at hands. You will be pointing at things, opening doors, and handing them keys. Clean hands. Trimmed nails. Not a complicated standard.

Breath under control. Coffee, cigarettes, last night's dinner — all of it shows up in the breath when you lean in to shake a hand or to show somebody a feature. Mints in the pocket. Use them.

None of that costs money. It costs attention. The salespeople who get this right are not the ones with the biggest closet. They are the ones who looked in a mirror before they left the house and asked one question: " Would I want to buy a car from the guy looking back at me?

The Mirror Test

That is the test. Before you walk out the door to start your shift, look at yourself as if a customer will be in about an hour.

Not the kind look. The customer looks. The look of someone who is already nervous about being on a car lot, bracing for what they expect to find, and about to make a quick judgment about you based on what they see.

Would they see someone who looks like they take this seriously? Or would they see someone who looks like he hopes nobody notices?

If the answer is the second one, fix it before you walk out. Not after the first customer of the day. Before. Because the first customer of the day is not going to give you a do-over.

The Catch

Here is the catch with appearance, and it is the catch that most training programs miss.

Appearance is necessary, but it is not sufficient. A salesperson who is sharply dressed but carries bad energy, wears a flat expression, or moves with desperation in his pace is going to fail the ten-second test anyway. Clean clothes will not make up for a bad presence. They are the floor, not the ceiling.

What appearance does is keep you from losing on a technicality. It puts you in the conversation. It removes one of the obvious reasons a customer would already be backing away. It does not, by itself, win anyone over.

That is why this is Chapter 3 and not Chapter 13. We are starting with the visible, controllable, fixable stuff. The stuff you can change tonight by ironing a shirt and getting a haircut. The harder work — the energy, the expression, the presence — comes in the chapters after this. But none of that work matters if you are losing the ten-second read on appearance alone.

Get this part right, and you are in the conversation. Get it wrong, and the conversation is over before it starts.

"The Rule: How you look is the first thing the customer reads, and they read it in less than a second. Showing up sharp does not win the sale by itself — but showing up sloppy can lose it before you say a word."

CHAPTER 4

ENERGY AND PRESENCE: WHAT YOU CARRY ONTO THE LOT

APPEARANCE IS WHAT THE customer sees.

Energy is what the customer feels.

Of the two, energy is harder to control, harder to fake, and more important. A sharply dressed salesperson with bad energy is going to lose the ten-second read every time to a plainly dressed salesperson with good energy. Customers can articulate why the first guy did not work for them — "he seemed off," "he made me uncomfortable," "something wasn't right" — but they cannot always tell you what it was. What it was was the energy. They felt something leaking out of him that did not match what his clothes were promising, and they trusted what they felt over what they saw.

Energy is the second loudest signal you send. It is the one that makes or breaks the ten-second window after appearance has gotten you in the door. And it is the one that nobody really teaches because nobody really knows how to teach it.

Let me try.

What Energy Actually Is

When I say 'energy,' I do not mean 'enthusiasm.' I do not mean pep. I am not telling you to bounce out onto the lot with a giant smile and a fist pump.

That is not energy — that is performance, and we already talked about how performed friendliness reads worse than no friendliness at all.

Energy is the internal state you are walking around in. It is whether you are calm or rattled. Present or distracted. Steady or jumpy. Glad to be there or grinding through a shift you wish was over. It is the condition of the person, not the act the person is putting on.

And here is the part that catches most salespeople off guard. The customer reads the condition, not the act.

You can put on the best smile in the world. If you are jumpy underneath, the customer will read you as jumpy. You can speak in the calmest voice you can manage. If you are frustrated underneath, the customer reads frustrated. The face and the voice are layers on top of the condition. The condition leaks through anyway.

That is why energy work is harder than appearance work. You cannot iron it. You cannot get a haircut for it. You have to actually be in the state you want the customer to feel.

What Leaks

Here is what is leaking from a salesperson with bad energy, and what the customer registers when it does.

Distraction. The salesperson who is half-thinking about the deal he is trying to save inside, half-thinking about the argument he had with his wife this morning, and half-thinking about how he is going to make rent — that is three halves, and there is no half left for the customer in front of him. The customer feels it. They feel like an interruption because they are.

Frustration. Maybe it is the manager. Maybe it is a slow morning. Maybe it is the deal that just fell apart in finance. The salesperson did not start the shift frustrated, but he is frustrated now, and he is walking out to meet a customer who has nothing to do with any of it. The customer reads the frustration as being aimed at them. They do not know it is not personal. To them, it just feels personal.

Boredom. Slow Tuesday. Third week of a slow month. The salesperson is going through the motions because that is all he has the bandwidth for. He looks bored. He sounds bored. And the customer thinks, "this person does not actually want to help me," and they are not wrong.

Desperation. The opposite of bored. The salesperson who has not closed a deal in two weeks and is white-knuckling the lot, hoping the next one is the one. Desperation reads as pressure before any pressure is applied. The customer feels the weight of the salesperson's need, and the customer is not in the business of carrying that weight.

Burnout. The veteran, who has been doing this for 10 years, has lost the joy of it. The customer in front of him is now a transaction, not a person. He is competent. He knows the script. But there is no life behind the eyes, and the customer can tell. They do not always know what is missing. They just know something is.

All of that leaks. None of it can be hidden with a smile.

What Good Energy Looks Like

The salesperson with good energy reads differently. The customer cannot always tell you why, but they can say the conversation felt easy because the salesperson seemed comfortable and did not make them feel pressured to keep talking.

Here is what is actually showing up when that happens.

Calm. Not flat. Not low-energy. Calm. The salesperson is not vibrating with stress. He is steady. He moves at a pace that suggests he is not in a hurry, but he is not dragging either. He can stand still without fidgeting. He can hold a pause without filling it.

Present. He is actually here. Not thinking about the last deal, not thinking about the next deal, not running a mental checklist in the background. This customer, this conversation, right now. The customer feels seen because they actually are being seen.

Open. His body is not closed off. His posture is loose. His hands are not balled up or stuffed away. There is room for the customer in the conversation — room to ask questions, room to push back, room to be uncertain. The salesperson does not seem to need anything from the interaction.

Steady. The energy does not spike when the customer says something promising and crashes when they say something discouraging. The salesperson stays where he is regardless of what the customer says. That steadiness is reassuring. It tells the customer this person is not riding their answers.

Patient. There is no rush behind the eyes. The customer can take a minute. They can think. They can not know what they want yet. The salesperson is fine with everything. That patience reads as professionalism, because it is.

Put all of that together, and you have a salesperson the customer wants to keep talking to. None of it required a great line. None of it required a sales technique. All of it was the condition the salesperson walked in carrying.

How to Actually Get There

This is the part people want answers to, and it is the part with no clean answers. You cannot read a chapter on energy and walk out with a fix, the way you can read a chapter on appearance and iron a shirt. But some things help.

Show up early. Five minutes early to a shift is not the same as on time. Five minutes early lets you walk in, breathe, settle in, look around, and get your head where it needs to be. On time means you walked in already rushed, and rushed energy stays with you for the first hour—customers in that first hour pay for that.

Take care of your body. I am not going to be your trainer. But I will tell you what 35 years on a lot tells you: the salesperson who is sleeping enough, eating something that is not just convenience-store food, and moving his body in some way during the week has different energy on the floor than the salesperson who is not. You cannot run on caffeine and stress forever and bring good energy to a customer. The body keeps score, and the customer reads the score.

Handle your own stuff. The argument with your wife. The late car payment. The kid who is struggling at school. Those are real, and they are not going away because you walked onto the lot. But if you have not done any work on them — if you are just stuffing them down and hoping they do not show — they show. Find a way to actually deal with what you are carrying. A walk. A phone call. A few minutes in your car to acknowledge that something is hard before you walk in. Pretending it is not there is not the same as handling it.

Reset between customers. Most salespeople drag the energy of one customer into the next one without realizing it. Bad customer walked away mad; you go right back out and meet the next pull-in, carrying all of that. Take thirty seconds. Get a glass of water. Shake out your shoulders. Put the last one down before you pick up the next one. Customers should not pay for the customer before them.

Watch yourself. The salespeople with the best energy are usually the ones who can name what their energy is like at any given moment. They check in. "Am I rushed? Am I tense? Am I distracted?" Awareness is most of the battle. You cannot adjust what you cannot see.

Energy Is Daily Work

Here is the thing about energy. It is not a skill you learn once. It is a condition you maintain. Every shift, every day, the energy you carry onto the lot is the energy customers are going to read. There is no version of this where you fix it once and never have to fix it again.

Which means the work of the ten-second rule is not in the ten seconds. It is in the hours, the days, the weeks before. It is in how you live, how you sleep. How do you handle the things that would otherwise leak out of you in front of a stranger? By the time a customer is walking toward you on the lot, the energy you are about to give them was set hours ago.

The salespeople who consistently win the ten-second read do not have a trick. They have a habit. They show up taking care of themselves, taking care of their head, and arriving at work ready to be present. That habit is what the customer is reading when they say the salesperson seemed easy to talk to.

Easy to talk to does not happen by accident. Easy to talk to is what good energy looks like from the outside.

"The Rule: Customers read your energy before they read your words — and your energy is set hours before you walk onto the lot.

Take care of what you carry in, because every customer is going to feel it."

CHAPTER 5

EXPRESSION: WHAT YOUR FACE SAYS BEFORE YOUR MOUTH OPENS

HERE IS A QUESTION almost no salesperson can answer honestly.

What does your face look like when you are not trying?

Not the smile you put on when you walk up to a customer. Not the look you give the manager when he asks how the morning is going. The face you wear when you are standing at the side of the showroom for thirty seconds with nothing to do. The face you carry as you walk across the lot, unaware that someone is watching—the default.

That default face is one of the most important things in this entire book. Because it is the face the customer sees first—and the face they read—before any of the faces you choose to wear ever come into play.

The Default Face Problem

Most people have no idea what their resting face looks like. They have spent their whole lives inside it, looking out through it, and they have never really seen it from the outside. They assume it looks pleasant. They assume it looks neutral. They assume it looks like nothing in particular.

It usually does not.

The default face on most adults reads as something. Sometimes it reads as tired. Sometimes it reads as annoyed. Sometimes it reads as worried, or impatient, or bored, or grim. The person wearing the face is not feeling any of those things—they are just standing there—but the face is still saying something, and the customer walking up is still reading it.

And here is the part that hurts. The customer reads the default face before they read the friendly face. The first split-second snapshot is the unguarded one. By the time the salesperson puts on the customer-facing expression, the impression has already been taken.

If the default face is open and easy, the impression that sticks is positive, and the friendly expression confirms it. If the default face is closed, hard, or distracted, the impression that locks in is negative, and the friendly expression on top of it reads as fake. The customer cannot articulate the mismatch, but they feel it. Something is off. The smile does not match what was there a second before.

What Faces Are Telling Customers

Here are the default faces I have seen on car lots for thirty-five years, and what they communicate to a customer who is already a little defensive.

The Death Stare. Hard eyes, locked jaw, not blinking enough. The salesperson is probably just bored or focused on something in his head. The customer reads aggression. Pressure incoming. Time to get the wallet hand ready to defend itself.

The Grimace. Mouth slightly turned down, brows pulled in. The salesperson is fine. He just has a face that pulls that way when relaxed. The customer reads displeasure, or worse, judgment. The customer wonders what they did wrong before they even got there.

The Checked-Out. Eyes a little glazed, mouth slack, face flat. The salesperson is daydreaming. The customer reads dead behind the eyes. They are now bracing to be processed by someone who would rather be anywhere else.

The Hover. The expression of someone watching too closely. Eyes locked on the customer from too far away, no softness around them. The salesperson is just paying attention. The customer reads predator. They actually flinch a little when the salesperson approaches.

The Forced Cheer. The face of someone who is constantly performing pleasantness because he has been told to. Mouth in a permanent half-smile, eyes that do not match. The customer reads insincerity. Whatever this person is selling isn't going to be straight.

None of those is the face the salesperson thinks he is wearing. All of them are the face the customer is seeing.

What an Open Face Actually Looks Like

Here is the face that wins the ten-second read. It is not a smile. Smiles can be faked, and a forced smile reads worse than no smile at all. It is something else.

Relaxed eyes. Not narrowed. Not wide. Soft at the edges, the way eyes are when a person is actually at ease.

Mouth that is at rest. Not pulled into a fake smile and not turned down. Just sitting in a neutral, slightly upturned position — the way a mouth sits on a person who is, in this moment, fine.

Loose jaw. A clenched jaw shows. A loose jaw shows differently. It registers as calm before the customer can name what they are seeing.

Brows that are not pulled in. Most worry shows in the brow before anywhere else. Brows that are level and easy to read, as if the person is not carrying anything heavy at that moment.

None of that is a smile. It is something more useful than a smile. It is the face of someone who is okay. Someone comfortable in his own skin. Someone the customer can read in half a second, and know will not be a problem to talk to.

A smile on top of that face is genuine and lands well. A smile on top of a tense face is the mismatch we already talked about, and it works against you.

Why You Cannot Just Smile Harder

This is the part I want to be clear about, because it is the part most sales training gets wrong.

"Smile when you greet the customer" is bad advice if the face underneath the smile is communicating something else. The customer is not reading the smile in isolation. They are reading the whole face. A smile sitting atop a clenched jaw and tense eyes reads as effortful, and effortful reads as untrustworthy. Whatever this person is showing me, he is showing me on purpose. What is he hiding?

The fix is not to smile more. The fix is to address the face underneath. To actually be the kind of person whose default expression is not communicating tension, fatigue, or boredom. The smile is then just the warm topcoat on a foundation that is already okay.

Which means the work on expression is not work you do in front of the customer. It is work you do on yourself. The condition we talked about in Chapter 4 — the energy that you walk in carrying — is the same condition that shows up on your face. You cannot have bad energy and a good resting face at the same time. They are the same thing.

How to Actually See Your Own Face

If you have read this far and you are still pretty sure your default face is fine, here is the test.

Set your phone to record video. Sit it on your desk. Walk in and out of the room a few times. Stand around. Look out a window. Check your watch. Do the things you do during the slow parts of a shift. Then go back and watch the footage with the sound off.

Watch your face when you do not know you are being watched. That is your default face. That is the one the customer sees in the first half-second when they pull onto the lot.

Most salespeople who do this for the first time are surprised. They thought they looked pleasant. They look tired. Or annoyed. Or like they would rather not be there. The face in their head does not match the one the camera caught.

That is the gap. That is what the customer is seeing. And the only way to close that gap is to know it exists, work on what is underneath it, and check yourself often enough that the default face stops working against you.

The Check Before You Walk Out

Here is the simplest practice I know. Right before you walk out to greet a customer — right before you step through the showroom door or out from behind the desk — do a quick three-part check.

Unclench your jaw. Most people do not realize they are holding their jaw until they let it go. Let it go.

Drop your shoulders. They are probably higher than they should be. Let them down.

Soften your eyes. Look at something in the middle distance, blink once, and let your eyes relax. Do not stare. Just settle.

That three-second reset takes a tense face and turns it neutral. A neutral face on top of decent energy is one the customer can read as someone okay to talk to. Which is what you are going for in the first ten seconds. You are not trying to dazzle them. You are trying to register as safe.

Safe is the bar. Safe is what gets you the conversation. Everything else — the rapport, the vehicle, the trade, the numbers — builds on a safe foundation. And safe starts in the face.

"The Rule: Your face is talking before your mouth is, and your default face is the one customers read first. Make sure what it is saying is something you would actually want said."

Chapter 6

The Look of Someone Who Wants to Help vs. Someone Who Wants to Sell

Customers can feel the difference between these two salespeople from across a parking lot.

They cannot always tell you what the difference is. They cannot point to a specific behavior. But they know which one is walking toward them, and they react accordingly. One they relax for. The other they brace for. The decision happens before the salesperson is close enough to say hello.

This chapter is about that difference. What it actually looks like. Why it matters more than almost anything else in the ten-second read. And how to be on the right side of it without faking your way there.

The Tell

Here is the cleanest way I can describe it.

The salesperson who wants to help looks like he is coming over to find out what the customer needs.

The salesperson who wants to sell looks like he is coming over to find out what the customer can be talked into.

Those are two completely different walks. Two completely different faces. Two completely different sets of eyes. And the customer reads them the same way they read every other thin-slice signal we have talked about — instantly, accurately, and without consciously deciding to.

The salesperson who wants to help is moving at a pace that says he has time for this. His face is open. His eyes are on the customer, but not locked on. His hands are loose. He looks like he is approaching a person.

The salesperson who wants to sell is leaning forward slightly. His eyes are already calculating. His mouth is set. His hands are sometimes balled up or pressed flat against his sides. He looks like he is approaching an opportunity. The customer is not a person to him at this moment. The customer is the next box to check.

That is the read. And once the customer has it, the conversation that follows is shaped by it. The customer who reads "help" opens up. The customer who reads "sell" closes down. Both readings happen in seconds, both readings stick, and both readings will determine what happens for the next forty-five minutes.

Where the Difference Comes From

The difference is not technique. Two salespeople can be taught the same opening line, the same approach, and the same body language, and one of them will still read as helping, and the other will still read as selling. The difference is underneath the technique. It is what the salesperson actually wants in the moment.

The salesperson who wants to help is, in that moment, genuinely curious about who the customer is and what they came in for. He has not decided yet how this conversation is going to go. He is open to it being anything. Maybe a buyer. Maybe a tire-kicker. Maybe a guy who is here to ask about service. He is okay with all of it because he is not attached to a specific outcome in the first ten seconds. He just wants to find out what is in front of him.

The salesperson who wants to sell is, in that moment, already partway through a sale that has not started yet. He has already decided whether this is a buyer or a non-buyer. He has already framed how he will play the conversation. He is not curious about who this person is. He is impatient to get to the part where he can use what he already knows.

That difference — the curious one versus the impatient one — is what shows up in the body, the face, the eyes, the pace, the energy. You cannot fake your way out of it because the customer is not reading the surface. They are reading the orientation underneath the surface. And the orientation below is either "what do you need" or "what can I close," and the customer can tell which one is in effect.

Why the Sell Posture Loses

Here is what most salespeople do not see clearly. The sell posture loses even when it succeeds. A customer who feels pressured during the ten-second read can occasionally still buy — the vehicle was right, the price was right, they were ready. But the experience leaves a residue. The buyer does not refer to the salesperson. Does not come back next time. Does not write a good review. The deal closed, but the relationship that would have led to the next deal never formed.

Multiply that over a career, and the cost is enormous. The salesperson who wins the sale and loses the customer has a very different career than the salesperson who wins both. One keeps replacing his pipeline from scratch every month. The other builds a book of business that compounds. And the difference between them often shows up in the ten seconds before anyone said a word.

Here is a story that shows what the sell posture looks like when it is loud.

FROM THE FLOOR

I was sitting in the front lobby of a dealership I managed — with a glass-front wall and a full view of the lot. A car pulled in. Two salespeople inside saw it at the same time. They both jumped up, ran for the door, and literally shoved each other, trying to get through it first, pushing and shoving like it was a race.

The customers, still in their car, watched every second of this.

The winner was out of breath when he got there. He stuck his hand out and started talking before he'd even caught his breath, never looked at the wife, never acknowledged the kids in the back seat. Just started in.

The family looked around for a few minutes and left.

When I asked what happened, the salesperson said: "They were just looking."

No. They were watching. And what they watched told them everything they needed to know about what the next hour would feel like. The sprint didn't just cost a deal; it cost a deal. It answered every one of the customer's silent questions about this place — and none of the answers were good.

Everything about that scene communicated 'sell,' not 'help.' The race to the door. The shoving. The arrival was out of breath. The hand stuck out before the customer had stepped out of the car. The wife and kids were ignored. None of it was about the family. All of it was about getting to the deal first.

The family read it accurately. They were not the priority. The race was the priority. And once that registered, they did the smart thing — they got out of there before the people racing to talk to them got close enough to do any real damage.

The salesperson's read on the situation was that the customers were just looking. The customers' read on the situation was that they did not want to be processed by a guy who was out of breath from elbowing his coworker out of the way to get to them first. Same event. Two completely different reads. The customer's read was what decided whether there was a deal.

How to Look Like Help

So how do you actually walk like someone who wants to help, not someone who wants to sell? You do not learn it from a script. But there are markers.

Pace. Calm and deliberate. Not slow. Not a stroll. But not a charge, either. The pace of a person who is glad to be heading toward this conversation but is not desperate to get there. If you can hear your own footsteps and they sound steady, you are about right. If you can feel your heart in your ears, you are moving too fast.

Eyes. On the customer, but soft. Not locked. You are looking at a person, not a target. Briefly notice the others with them — wife, kids, friend. Acknowledge they exist. Eyes that scan only the buyer and skip everyone else read as transactional. Eyes that take in the whole group read as human.

Hands. Loose. Visible. Not clenched. Not crossed. Not stuffed in pockets in a way that looks closed off. A hand at your side is fine. A hand with a folder or a clipboard held naturally is fine. A hand that looks like it is about to spring forward for the shake is too much.

Mouth. Closed but soft. The mouth that is about to say something easy. Not the mouth that's already mid-pitch. Lips loose. The space between you and the customer is a space the customer should feel welcome to step into—not a space you are filling before they get a chance.

Opening line. Short. Friendly. No question that requires them to commit to anything. "Hey, welcome in. Take your time — just let me know when you have a question." That is helpful. "What are you looking to buy today?" is a selling question. Same situation. Different read. The first one opens the door. The second one slams it shut while pretending to open it.

The Internal Move

All of the above is the outside. But the outside follows the inside, and the inside is one question you ask yourself before you walk out.

"What does this person need from me right now?"

Not "what can I get out of this?" Not "is this a buyer?" Not "how do I move this toward a test drive?" Just — what does this person need from me right now? Even if you do not have the answer yet. Even if the honest answer is "I do not know, I have to find out." The question itself reorients you. It puts you on the help side of the line before you have taken a step.

The salespeople who consistently win the ten-second read are the ones who can hold that question in their head all the way through the approach. They are not pretending to care. They are actually curious. Whatever they find out about the customer in the next few minutes will determine what happens next. They have not pre-decided. They are open.

Customers feel the difference because there is a difference. Help and sell are two different orientations that show up in everything from the pace of the walk to the angle of the head. Get the orientation right, and most of the surface details fall into place on their own. Get the orientation wrong, and no amount of surface coaching can hide it.

"The Rule: The customer can tell the difference between a salesperson who wants to help and one who wants to sell — from across the lot, before anyone speaks. Walk out with the right question in your head and the right one will show on your face."

CHAPTER 7

THE TEN-SECOND READ: HOW CUSTOMERS DECIDE WHO YOU ARE

S O FAR, WE HAVE talked about what the customer is reading and what they are seeing. This chapter is about the part underneath that. The decision they are actually making.

Because the customer is not just registering signals. They are using those signals to answer a specific question. And the question is not the one most salespeople think it is.

The Question They Are Actually Asking

The customer's brain in the first ten seconds is not asking, "Is this a good salesperson?" It is not asking "does this person know the inventory?" It is not even asking, "Am I going to buy a car from this person?"

It is asking something more basic.

"Is this person safe to talk to?"

That is the question. And it is the question for a reason. The customer arrived defensive. They arrived expecting some version of unpleasant. The thing they are scanning for first is whether the unpleasant they were braced for is about to happen. Safety is the first decision. Everything else — trust, interest, willingness to engage — builds on top of it.

Most salespeople skip this layer entirely. They walk out trying to be impressive, or knowledgeable, or friendly, when the customer has not yet decided on the more basic thing. They are answering questions the customer has not yet gotten to, while leaving unanswered the only question the customer is actually asking right now.

Safe first. Then everything else.

What "Safe" Means Here

I want to be careful with that word, because it sounds soft, and this is not a soft point.

Safe, in the ten-second window, does not mean physically safe. The customer is not afraid that you will attack them. Safe means something more specific.

Safe means this person won't make me feel stupid.

Safe means this person won't push me into anything.

Safe means this person is not going to make me waste my afternoon.

Safe means this person isn't going to try to humiliate me about my credit, trade, or budget.

Safe means this person is going to let me think, let me say no, and let me leave if I need to.

That is the safety the customer is scanning for. And every one of those concerns is in their head when they pull onto the lot. They are not making it up. Most of them have a story that justifies it. The brother-in-law who got worked over. The time they got pressured into a payment they could not afford. The time a salesperson looked at their credit and gave them the face. They are scanning your face, your walk, your eyes, your pace for evidence that this time will be the same—or different.

The Three Decisions in the First Ten Seconds

Underneath the safety question, the customer is actually making three decisions, often in this order, often within seconds of each other.

First decision: Is this person a threat to my comfort? Are they going to be loud, pushy, aggressive, in my face? The customer reads pace, posture, and expression for the answer. A calm, measured approach answers in the negative. A sprint answers yes.

Second decision: Will this person respect me? Are they going to take me seriously, listen to what I actually want, and treat me like an adult with a brain? The customer reads eye contact, the opening line, and whether you acknowledged the people with them. Looking past the wife to talk to the husband yields no answer. Greeting both of them answers yes.

Third decision: Is this person going to be honest with me? Are they straight, or are they going to play games? The customer reads micro-signals — whether your face matches your words, whether your eyes are steady, whether there is a hint of performance under what you are saying. A genuine, simple greeting answers yes. A scripted, polished one answers no, because polished reads as practiced, and practiced reads as performance.

Three decisions. All made before you have said more than a sentence. All locked in by the time you finish your opening line. And all carried into the next forty-five minutes, whether you do anything about them or not.

Why You Cannot Argue Your Way Out of It

Here is the cruel part. If the customer's ten-second read comes out negative on any of those three decisions, you cannot fix it by talking more. Talking more usually makes it worse. The customer who has decided you are a threat to their comfort will hear every additional word as more of a threat. The customer who has decided you do not respect them will hear your friendliness as condescension. The customer who has decided you are not going to be honest will read every sentence for the catch.

Words spoken into a bad ten-second read do not undo the read. They confirm it. The customer is now finding evidence for what they already decided, not reconsidering the decision.

That is why the ten-second read is so important. It is not just the first impression. It is the lens through which everything that follows is viewed. Get the read right, and your words land. Get the reading wrong, and your words become more reasons for the customer to leave.

How to Pass the Three Decisions

If the customer is making three decisions in the first ten seconds, the question is how to land on the right side of each one. Here is the short version.

To pass the threat-to-comfort decision, move slowly. Do not crowd. Keep your voice in a normal register. Do not start with a sales question. Start with a welcome. "Hey, welcome in," not "What are you looking to buy?" The first one is hospitality. The second one is interrogation. The customer can tell the difference.

To pass the respect decision, see everyone. The buyer is whoever brought them in, but they rarely make the decision alone. Wife. Husband. Kids. A friend who came along. Look at all of them. Speak to all of them. Acknowledge the kid in the back seat. Acknowledge the friend. The customer who came in for the car is also the spouse, the parent, or the friend of the person beside them. Treat them like a whole person, and you have passed the respect test before you try.

To pass the honesty decision, do less. Less polish. Less performance. Less pitch. A simple greeting in your own voice sounds more honest than a polished one in your sales voice. The customer is not looking for a great opening line. They are looking for a real person. Be the real person, and the decision goes your way.

None of those moves is complicated. None of them requires special training. All of them require you to know what the customer is actually deciding in those first ten seconds, so you can speak to those decisions instead of speaking past them.

The Customer Has Already Decided

By the time your opening line is finished, the three decisions are locked in. The conversation that follows will operate within the frame that those decisions created.

If you passed all three, you are now talking to a customer who is open, attentive, and willing to be guided. That customer will tell you what they came in for. They will let you ask questions. They will follow your lead to the right vehicle, the right test drive, the right conversation about numbers. The sale with that customer feels easy because the customer isn't fighting you.

If you failed one or more of them, you are now talking to a customer who is closed, guarded, and looking for an exit. That customer will say they are just looking. They will give you nothing to work with. They will count the minutes until they can politely leave. The sale that does not happen with that customer also feels easy, in the sense that it ended quickly. But it ended for reasons set in the first ten seconds, not for anything to do with the car, the price, or the offer.

The customer made their decision about you fast. Faster than they meant to. Faster than you knew. Your job is to know what those decisions are, what they are based on, and how to land on the right side of each one. Because once they are made, they are very hard to unmake.

"The Rule: In the first ten seconds, the customer is not deciding whether to buy a car. They are deciding whether you are safe, respectful, and honest. Win those three, and the rest of the conversation has a chance. Lose any one of them and the rest is just stalling."

CHAPTER 8

WHEN THE FIRST IMPRESSION IS ALREADY WRONG

SOMETIMES YOU KNOW. THIRTY seconds in, before any real conversation has started, you can feel it.

The customer is not opening up. Their answers are clipped. Their eyes are not meeting yours. Their body is angled toward the exit. The wife is closer to the husband than she was when they got out of the car. Everything about the read says this is not going well, and you have not done anything yet.

Something went wrong. The first impression was negative, and you are now operating from a deficit. Before we talk about how to recover — that is, the next chapter — we need to talk about what just happened. Because if you do not know what went wrong, you cannot fix it. And if you cannot read when it is wrong, you will not even know there is something to fix.

The Signs You Already Lost the Read

Customers do not always tell you that the first impression went badly. They seldom do, in fact. They are not going to look you in the eye and say, "I did not like the way you walked up." They are too polite. They were raised better than that. Instead, they show you, and you have to know what to look for.

The clipped answer. You asked an open question. They gave a one-word reply. "What brings you in?" "Just looking." That is not just the standard brush-off. That is a customer who has already decided to give you nothing. The brush-off line is the symptom. The decision happened in the ten-second window before they spoke.

The angled body. The customer's shoulders are not square to you. They are turned slightly toward the car they pulled up in, or toward the exit, or toward their spouse. The angle tells you their body is already preparing to leave, even as their mouth remains polite.

The absent eye contact. They are not looking at you. They are looking at the car. The pavement. Their phone. Their spouse. Their feet. An open customer will make eye contact a few times in the first 30 seconds. A closed customer will not. The eyes are one of the loudest signals, and once they are not on you, they are telling you the read is bad.

The drift. They are stepping away from you while you are talking. Half an inch, then another half inch, then a full step. They are not consciously deciding to back up. Their body is just creating distance because their gut is telling them to. Watch the feet.

The spousal lean. The wife steps closer to the husband, or the husband steps closer to the wife. They are gathering up and forming a small unit. That is what people do when they feel they are about to leave together. It happens before they consciously decide to go.

The flat thank-you. You said something. They said, "Okay, thanks." That two-word reply, said flat, is the verbal equivalent of a closed door. It is not impolite. It is not aggressive. It is just done. They have already decided to disengage.

Most salespeople miss all of these signals because they are still listening to their own opening line and waiting for the customer to respond "correctly." They are watching for the right words to come out of the customer's mouth, when the customer's whole body has already given them the answer.

The body talks first. The body talks loudest. Read the body.

Why It Happened

The hard part about diagnosing a bad first impression is that you usually cannot point to one thing. It is rarely a single mistake. It is the accumulation of signals — the appearance, the pace, the expression, the energy, the eye contact — that together add up to a negative read.

But there are some common patterns. Patterns I have watched cost deals for thirty-five years. If the read came out badly, it is usually one of these.

You came on too fast. Pace too quick. Closing the distance too eagerly. The customer's nervous system registered urgency, and urgency reads as pressure. Their guard came up before you got within ten feet.

You came on too eagerly. Big smile too early. Eye contact too intense. Voice pitched a little too friendly. The customer's gut said "this is performance," and performance reads as manipulation, even when none was intended.

You missed someone. You greeted the husband and not the wife. The wife and not the husband. The buyer and not the kid in the back. The whole party, but not the one who is actually the decision-maker. Whoever you missed is now operating from a deficit, and they will pull the rest of the group with them.

You opened with a question they did not want to answer. "What are you looking to buy?" "What's your budget?" "Are you trading something in?" Those are working questions, and they are fine, ten or fifteen minutes into a conversation. As an opener, they tell the customer this is going to be a sales process before the customer has even decided to be in one.

You looked at them wrong. Not how you think. Eyes that lingered too long. Eyes that did not linger long enough. Eyes that flicked to their car, their clothes, their shoes — anywhere that signaled you were sizing them up. The customer read it, even if they could not say what they read, and they backed off.

Something about you was off, and you did not know it. The shirt was wrinkled, and you did not notice. The breath was bad, and you did not notice. The walk was a little too fast, and you didn't notice. The expression on your face when you came out of the building was not the expression you thought you were wearing. Any one of those, all by itself, can cost the ten-second read. And the cruel part is that you usually do not know which one it was.

When It Is Not You

This is important, and I want to say it plainly. Sometimes the bad first impression is not yours.

Sometimes the customer arrived already closed. Bad day. Bad mood. Bad history with car dealerships. The salesperson at the last lot was the one who did the damage, and you are now walking into the wake of that experience. You did nothing wrong, and the customer will still be hard to open.

Sometimes, something specific in your appearance or demeanor, through no fault of your own, reminds the customer of someone they do not like. We have a story about that later in this book. The wrong eyes. The wrong voice. The wrong build. None of it is anything you did. All of it is going to make the conversation harder anyway.

Sometimes the customer has a story going on that has nothing to do with you. Their mother is sick. Their kid is in trouble. Their job is in jeopardy. They came to look at a car because their lease is up, not because they wanted to be here. Their closed posture has nothing to do with the salesperson. It is just where they are today.

The reason this matters is that you cannot fix what is not yours to fix. If you assume every bad first impression is your fault and try to compensate, you will overcorrect. You will get pushier. Try harder. Smile bigger. All of which makes a bad situation worse — because if the bad read is theirs, not yours, your extra effort reads as pressure on top of whatever they were already carrying.

The skill is to read whether you broke it or whether you walked into it already broken. The signals you used to diagnose them in the ten-second window are the same ones you use here. The difference is the trajectory. If they got closer during your approach, it is probably partly you. If they were closed the second they got out of the car — if they never opened, never relaxed, never met your eyes from the start — you walked into something that was already in place.

Sitting With It

Here is the move that most salespeople cannot make. They cannot just sit with the fact that the first impression went sideways.

They feel it goes badly, and they panic. They try to talk over it. They double down on the line they were about to use. They get louder, more polished, more salesman-like. All of which makes the read worse, because it confirms the customer's suspicion that this is what they walked into.

The first thing to do when you realize the first impression is wrong is to stop digging. Stop talking. Slow down. Let there be a pause. The salesperson who is willing to stand in a thirty-second silence with a customer who has gone cold is the salesperson who has any chance at all of resetting the read. The salesperson who fills every silence with more pitching is digging the hole deeper.

The pause is uncomfortable. Sit in it anyway, because the next chapter is about what to do with that pause — how actually to reset a bad first impression. But you cannot reset what you have not first acknowledged. And you cannot acknowledge it if you are still trying to plow forward as if it did not happen.

The first move when the read goes wrong is to recognize it. To see it, to name it to yourself, to stop running the original plan. Everything that follows depends on that one move.

Read the body. Trust what you see. And stop the bleeding before you try to do anything else.

"The Rule: When the first impression goes wrong, the customer's body will tell you long before their mouth does. Read the signals, stop talking, and admit to yourself what happened — because you cannot fix what you refuse to see."

Chapter 9

Resetting a Bad First Impression

THE LAST CHAPTER ENDED on a pause. The bad first impression has landed, you have seen it land, and now you are standing in front of a customer whose body has already turned slightly toward the exit.

This chapter is about what to do next.

I want to say up front that resetting a bad first impression is harder than recovering from a bad approach. Book 5 covered the approach—the walk, the distance, the opening line. If the approach went sideways, the customer can still be brought back, because the approach is a technique, and techniques can be adjusted in real time. The first impression is something more basic. It is the gut read, locked in fast, sitting deep. It will not be undone by a better opening line two minutes in. It has to be undone differently.

But it can be undone. I have seen it happen many times. I have done it many times. Here is how.

The Reset Window

A bad first impression has a reset window. The window is short, but it exists, and most salespeople do not even know it is there.

The window is usually the next 30 to 60 seconds after you realize the first impression went wrong. Past that, the read has fully set, the customer is mentally rehearsing their exit, and the chances of recovery drop fast. Inside the window, you have a real shot—if you make the right move.

The wrong move is to try harder. To smile bigger. To get more polished. To push the original plan with more energy. All of that confirms the read instead of resetting it. The customer reads it as the salesperson doubling down, which comes across as desperate, which is exactly what they were afraid of when they pulled in.

The right move is the opposite. To drop the original plan, lower the energy, and acknowledge — in your body, in your face, in your voice — that the situation needs a different opening than the one you walked in with.

Here Is What That Actually Looks Like

First, you stop talking. If you were mid-pitch, end the sentence and stop. The reset cannot start until the original line is closed out. Customers who are getting talked at by a salesperson who senses he is losing them are not getting a reset; they are getting a more intense version of what was already failing.

Second, you create space. Take a small step back. Not a retreat. A loosening. Bring the physical distance back to a comfortable conversational range. If you were leaning in, square up and stand normally. The body language tells the customer this is no longer the moment you thought it was.

Third, you change the tone. The voice you came in with was the sales voice, greeting voice, or whatever voice you had been using with customers all day. Drop it. The voice you want now is the voice you would use when talking to a neighbor at the mailbox. Lower. Slower. Less polished. More human.

Fourth, you acknowledge something real. This is the move. This is the one most salespeople will not make. You name the thing that is in the room. Not the bad impression itself — you do not say "I feel like this is going badly." You name whatever real thing is shaping the moment. The heat. The traffic they fought to get there. The fact that you can tell they have probably done a lot of looking already today. The fact that you noticed they have kids waiting in the car.

Whatever it is, naming a real thing in the moment is what tells the customer you are paying attention to them as a person, not running a script. That single moment can break the read. It does not always. But it can.

And it is the only move that has a real chance of breaking it inside that thirty-to-sixty-second window.

A Live Example

Here is what this looks like in actual practice.

FROM THE FLOOR

The summer heat in Texas is no joke. I was managing a used-car lot — no air conditioning on the lot, obviously — and it was one of those July afternoons when the asphalt is soft, and the air feels like a wet towel. A couple pulled in. I watched my newest salesperson sprint out to meet them — which was already the wrong move — and by the time he got to them, he was visibly sweating through his shirt. The customers looked at him, looked at each other, and said they were just looking. He came back inside looking defeated.

I went out. Introduced myself. Said: "Sorry about the heat — let me know if you want to step inside and cool off while we talk." That's all it took. They came inside. We sold them a car in ninety minutes. The first salesperson did everything wrong before he said a word. I did one thing right: I acknowledged where they were before I asked anything of them.

Look at what happened there. The first salesperson didn't just fail the ten-second read—he confirmed every single thing customers were already worried about. He came at them too fast. He arrived out of breath. He was visibly uncomfortable. He looked desperate. By the time he opened his mouth, the customers had already decided how this was going to go, and they did the smart thing and said they were just looking.

I walked out with no special technique. I did not have a great opening line. I did not even ask them about the car. What I did was acknowledge the one thing that was unavoidably in the room — the heat — and offer them something that put their comfort ahead of my agenda. Inside the air-conditioned showroom. While we talk. Two small pieces. The first acknowledged a real thing. The second made clear there was no rush.

That was the reset. That was the move that broke the read the first salesperson had locked in. The customers walked inside, sat down, and the conversation that followed was the conversation that should have happened from the start.

Notice what I did not do. I did not apologize for the first salesperson. I did not explain or excuse him. I did not even mention him. The customers had already filed him away in the "that was unpleasant" folder, and bringing him back up would just have reactivated the bad read. The reset works best when it does not draw attention to what went wrong. It just offers a different door.

What Acknowledgment Sounds Like

The acknowledgment line is the single most important move in a reset, so let me give you more examples of what it can sound like. None of these are scripts. All of them are templates for the kind of language that breaks a bad read.

"Sorry about the heat — let me know if you want to step inside and cool off while we talk."

"Looks like you all have done some looking already today. Take your time — I'm around if you have a question."

"Hey, I know how this usually goes — take your time, walk around, and if you want me, I'm right over here."

"Welcome in. No pressure either way — you want me to come back over in a few minutes, or do you want just to look first?"

"Traffic getting in was rough today — glad you made it. Take your time, I'm here when you need me."

What all of those have in common is that they put the customer's comfort ahead of your agenda, and they do it in plain language, in a normal voice, with no hook or close attached. They are not setting up the next move. They are creating space. The customer who hears a line like that hears something different than what they were braced for, and the read begins to soften almost immediately.

When the Reset Does Not Work

Sometimes the reset does not work. The customer was too far closed when you got there, or whatever they were carrying when they pulled in was bigger than what one acknowledgment can move, or the timing was just wrong. They thank you politely, and they leave anyway.

That is going to happen. It is part of the business. The reset is not a magic trick. It is a move that gives you a real chance when the alternative was a guaranteed loss.

What you do not do is push when the reset does not land. If you offer the acknowledgment and the customer is still facing the exit, let them go. You say something like "Totally understand — here's my card if anything looks interesting, or if you want to come back another day." And you mean it. You do not chase. You do not try to recover the recovery.

Because here is the long game. A customer who leaves on a polite note often comes back. Maybe today. Maybe tomorrow. Maybe in three months, when their lease is up. The salesperson who let them leave with their dignity intact is the salesperson they remember. The one who chased them down the lot trying to save the deal is the salesperson they tell their friends to avoid.

A graceful exit is also part of the reset. Maybe the most important part.

The Reset Is About Them, Not You

Here is the underlying principle, and I was hoping you could hold on to it when you walk out tomorrow.

The reset is not about saving the deal. It is about treating the customer like a person whose comfort matters more than your shift goal.

If you make the move to save the deal, it comes out wrong. The customer reads the desperation under it, and the reset fails. If you make the move because you genuinely want them to feel okay in your presence — even if they end up leaving — it comes out clean and has a real chance of working.

That paradox is the secret of the reset. The salespeople who can reset bad first impressions are the ones willing to lose the deal in the service of treating the customer well, which sounds backward. But over a career, those are also the salespeople who lose the fewest deals in the long run. Because customers can tell when they are being treated like a person, and they remember it.

The reset is a small moment. Thirty seconds. A few words. But inside that small moment is everything this book is about. Knowing what the customer is feeling. Knowing what they are reading. Knowing which move actually addresses what they are reading and being willing to make that move, even when the easier thing is to keep talking and hope.

Hope is not a strategy. The reset is a strategy. Use it.

"The Rule: A bad first impression can be reset — but only by dropping the original plan, acknowledging something real in the moment, and putting the customer's comfort ahead of your agenda. The salesperson who is willing to lose the deal to do that is the salesperson who recovers the most of them."

CHAPTER 10

THE TEN-SECOND RULE IN THE SHOWROOM

S O FAR, WE HAVE been mostly talking about the lot. The customer is pulling in. The salesperson walked out. The ten-second window forming on a piece of asphalt under a Texas sun.

But not every customer arrives that way. Some of them walk in through the front door. They parked outside, walked across the lot themselves, pushed the door open, and stepped into the showroom. And the moment that door closes behind them, the ten-second rule starts running on the inside of the building — with a different set of variables and a different set of people they are reading.

The showroom is its own kind of test. And most dealerships fail it without realizing they are.

What the Customer Sees Walking In

Stand inside any showroom and watch what happens when a customer walks in. Do not watch the customer. Watch what the customer is watching.

They are scanning. Just like they did on the lot, their eyes are moving fast across the room, taking in every signal at once, and they are running the same thin-slice assessment we talked about in Chapter 1. Only now the assessment is not about one salesperson. It is about the whole room.

Here is the inventory of what is registering.

Who looked up. The customer walks in and immediately notices which heads turned. Did the receptionist make eye contact? Did anyone else acknowledge them? Or did the entire room treat the door opening like a gust of wind? An unacknowledged entry tells the customer they are not a priority. A room full of people who all looked up briefly and went back to their work tells the customer they were seen, which is something different and much better.

Who looked up and how. There is a difference between a head that turned because someone heard the door and went back to typing, and a head that turned and held the look for an extra second because the person was actually checking who walked in. The customer reads that difference. The first one feels like indifference. The second one feels like attention. And then there is the third version — the head that snapped up and the eyes that locked on like a predator. That one reads as someone about to pounce, which is worse than the indifference. Aim for the middle.

The energy of the room. Conversations are happening in normal voices. Phones are ringing and being answered. Salespeople at desks doing actual work. That registers as a real business. By contrast, a room full of salespeople standing in clusters laughing too loudly, or all hunched over phones, or eerily silent and staring — those all register as something off. The customer cannot always name what is off. They just feel the room is wrong before they have stepped fully inside.

The condition of the place. Floors are clean or not. Desks organized or not. Display vehicles on the floor, polished or dusty. The bathroom door was propped open with a trash bag. The empty coffee carafe is sitting on a stained counter. None of it is the customer's problem to solve. All of it is shaping the read they take in those first ten seconds. The customer who walks into a showroom that looks well cared for feels they are in the hands of people who take care of things. The customer who walks into a showroom that looks neglected feels they are in the hands of people who neglect things.

The first interaction. The first voice that says hello — whoever it is — sets the tone for the whole visit. If it is the receptionist with a warm, easy

"Welcome in," the customer's shoulders drop. If it is a salesperson hurrying across the showroom, calling out before they have crossed the floor, the customer's shoulders go up. The same words can be read totally differently depending on who is saying them, how, and from how far away.

The Walk-In Customer Is Different

Here is something most salespeople miss. The walk-in customer is a different animal from the lot customer.

The lot customer pulled up, looked around outside, and was either greeted or not. They made one decision — to get out of the car. They are still in their car if they have not made that decision yet, which gives them the option to drive away unseen.

The walk-in customer has already made more decisions. They drove in. They parked. They got out. They walked across the lot. They opened the door. They stepped inside. That is six decisions in their favor before any salesperson said a word. The walk-in customer is, by definition, more committed than the lot customer.

Which means two things. First, the bar for a successful ten-second read is actually higher with a walk-in, because the customer has already invested more. They came in expecting something to happen. If nothing does — if the room is dead, if nobody looks up, if no one greets them — the disappointment is bigger, and the read is worse. Their investment was higher; the failure is more visible.

Second, the walk-in customer is often closer to a sale than the salesperson assumes. They did not stop at the curb. They did not sit in the parking lot. They came in. Treat the walk-in like they might be ready to buy today, because a high percentage of them are. The salesperson who assumes the walk-in is just looking is going to greet them like a tire-kicker, and the walk-in is going to feel that assumption and act accordingly.

Showroom Culture Is the Tell

Here is the part most salespeople cannot fix on their own, and it has to be said anyway.

The ten-second read on a showroom is a read on the dealership's culture, not the skill of any one salesperson. The customer is reading the whole room. Whoever is in the room — the receptionist, the porters, the other salespeople, the managers walking through — all of them are contributing to the read whether they know it or not.

If the showroom culture is good — if people generally look up when the door opens, if greetings happen quickly, if voices stay in a normal range, if the place looks taken care of, if everyone seems to know their job and be doing it — then the walk-in customer's read comes out positive before any one salesperson has done anything. The room did the work.

If the showroom culture is bad — if heads do not turn, if greetings get delayed, if voices are too loud or too quiet, if the room looks neglected, if salespeople are visibly avoiding the door — then the walk-in customer's read comes out negative, no matter how good the one salesperson is who eventually walks over. That salesperson is now working against a read-the-room created.

That is why the showroom test is harder. One person cannot pass it alone. The room either passes or it does not. And if it does not, the salespeople in that room are spending every walk-in trying to overcome the deficit the room created.

What You Can Do Anyway

That said, you cannot control the whole room. You can only control your part of it. So here is what your part of it looks like.

Be the head that turns. When the door opens, look up. Every time. Not a stare. A glance, a small acknowledgment, then back to whatever you were doing. That one second of being seen changes the customer's read of the room, even if you are not the one who greets them.

Be the voice. If you are the closest salesperson to the door and no one else has acknowledged them yet, you are the greeter. Do not wait for the rotation. Do not wait for the receptionist. Stand up, walk over at a normal pace, and welcome them in. The customer who has been standing in a showroom for twenty seconds with no acknowledgment has had time to start backing toward the door. Twenty seconds is forever when you are unacknowledged.

Keep your own corner sharp. The desk you work at is part of the showroom. The customer can see it. Coffee cup rings on the surface, paperwork piled randomly, a personal phone face up next to a name plate — all of it shows. Keep your desk like a place where business gets done. That part is fully yours to control.

Be aware of what you sound like to a stranger. The conversation you are having with another salesperson—the customer can hear it. The joke you are making at the front desk — the customer can hear it. The phone call you are on — if your voice is louder than it needs to be, the customer can hear it. Anything happening in the room is visible from the walk-in. Behave accordingly.

Talk to the room when you can. If you have any influence over how the team handles walk-ins — if you are a senior salesperson, a team lead, anyone with a voice — use it. Make sure the team knows that heads turn when the door opens. The receptionist greets first. Those greetings happen within ten seconds. That the room is on, not off. The salesperson who works only in his own corner of the showroom is leaving the rest of his potential customers on the table. The salesperson who works in the room is multiplying his own results.

The Showroom Within Ten Seconds

In ten seconds, here is what a walk-in customer needs to register in a healthy showroom.

They were noticed. At least one head turned and acknowledged the door.

They were greeted. By the receptionist, by a salesperson, by anyone whose job it was to greet them — within those first ten seconds, somebody said a version of "welcome in."

They were not pounced on. The greeting was warm but not aggressive. They had room to look around, to step further inside, to orient themselves before any salesperson was directly in their path.

They saw a room that took itself seriously. Clean. Organized. The kind of place where business gets done.

They felt the energy of the room as a normal working business. Not chaotic. Not dead. Not weirdly silent. Just a place doing its work.

If a walk-in customer registers all five of those in the first ten seconds, the rest of the visit has a runway. The salesperson who eventually sits down with them is meeting a customer whose guard is already lower than it would be outside. That is a customer who will talk, listen, share information, and let the conversation develop.

If they register none of them, the salesperson who eventually sits down with them is sitting down with a customer whose decision to leave has already begun to form. That salesperson can be the best in the business and still walk out of the meeting empty-handed, because the read on the room was already locked in before they got involved.

The ten-second rule does not stop at the front door. It walks the customer through it. The salesperson who understands that is the one who watches the door, watches the room, and watches the small signals that decide whether a walk-in becomes a deal or just someone who looked around for two minutes and quietly left.

"The Rule: The walk-in customer reads the whole room in ten seconds, not just the salesperson. If you cannot fix the room, fix your corner of it — and be the head that turns when the door opens."

CHAPTER 11

THE TEN-SECOND RULE ON THE PHONE

YOU CANNOT SEE A voice. But you can read one.

Everything we have been talking about in this book — the thin-slice read, the safety question, the three decisions — happens just as quickly on the phone as in person. Maybe faster. Because the customer on the other end of the line has only one input to work with, and that one input is going to carry all of the work that, in person, would have been spread across face, body, pace, and presence. The voice is doing everything.

The ten-second rule on the phone is real, and the salespeople who treat it like a lesser medium are losing deals before they ever know they had a shot.

The First Three Seconds

On the phone, the ten-second window is actually shorter. The customer makes their first read in the first three to five seconds. Sometimes inside the first word.

Think about it from their side. They dial. The phone rings. Someone picks up. That someone says something. The customer's gut produces a feeling about someone before the sentence is finished. They have already decided whether they are in good hands or not, whether this person is a professional or a phone answerer, and whether they want to continue or hang up and try another dealership.

All of it in the first sentence. Sometimes on the first syllable.

Which means how you answer the phone matters more than most salespeople realize. The opening greeting is not a formality. It is the entire first impression compressed into one breath. Get it wrong, and you have already lost ground, so the next ten minutes will be spent trying to recover. Get it right, and you are starting from a position the customer trusts before they have heard your name.

What the Customer Reads in a Voice

Here is what the customer's ear is picking up in those first few seconds. Most of it operates below conscious awareness, exactly like the visual thin-slice on the lot. The customer is not analyzing your voice. They are reacting to it.

Tone. The pitch and warmth of the voice. A flat tone reads as bored. A clipped tone reads as annoyed. A too-cheerful tone reads as fake. The voice that wins is somewhere in the middle — warm enough to feel human, steady enough to feel professional, easy enough to feel genuine.

Pace. How fast are you talking? Salespeople under pressure talk fast. They are trying to get information out, control the call, and move toward the appointment. The customer hears the speed and reads it as pressure. Slow down. A relaxed pace at the start of the call signals to the customer that this is a conversation, not a closing attempt.

Volume. Too loud reads as aggressive. Too quiet reads as uncertain. The middle is the volume of a normal in-person conversation — the volume you would use if the person were sitting two feet from you, not the volume of someone projecting across a room.

Energy. Yes, you can hear energy through a phone. The salesperson who is genuinely glad someone called sounds different from the one grinding through a shift and resenting the ring. The customer cannot tell you what the difference is, but they hear it instantly. The bored voice answers the call, and the customer is already half out.

Pause use. Some salespeople fill every silence on a phone call. They cannot let air sit in the line for a second without rushing to fill it with words. The customer reads that as nervous. The salesperson who can hold a brief pause — long enough to actually think about what was just said — reads as composed. Composure on the phone is rare. Customers notice it.

Listening to sounds. The small sounds that tell the customer you are still there and paying attention. Quiet "mm-hm," "okay," "right." Not every other word. Just enough to tell the customer their voice is reaching a human being who is taking it in. The dead silence on the other end of a phone is unnerving. The over-affirming "absolutely-totally-yes" every two seconds is exhausting. Aim for the present without being performative.

How to Answer the Phone

Here is the simplest possible standard for answering a phone in a dealership.

Answer in three rings or fewer. Not because three is magic, but because every ring past three makes the caller wonder if anyone is going to pick up. A caller who has wondered if anyone is going to pick up has already had their first negative read, before any voice comes on the line.

Use the same greeting every time, and make sure it has three parts. The name of the dealership. Your name. An offer of help. Something like: "Thanks for calling [Dealership]. This is [Your Name]. How can I help you?" That is it. No more. No less. Said in a normal voice at a normal pace.

Notice what is missing. No fake enthusiasm. No "happy to assist you today!" No singsong tone. No script-voice. The greeting works because it is short, complete, and delivered as if a real person had picked up the phone. That alone separates you from most of what customers hear when they call around.

And then — and this is the part most salespeople rush — stop. Let the customer talk. Do not jump in. Do not anticipate. They called for a reason. Let them tell you what it is, in their own words, at their own pace.

The Smile Test

Old phone trick that turns out to be real. Smile while you are answering the phone. The voice carries it.

A smile changes the shape of the mouth. It changes the shape of the breath. It changes the voice's resonance. The person on the other end of the line cannot see your face, but they can hear the difference between a voice from a relaxed, slightly smiling face and one from a flat, tired face. The first one reads as welcoming. The second one reads as a chore.

This is not about performing happiness. We have been clear that performed happiness reads as fake. The smile here is small and natural — the kind of mouth shape that goes with actually being glad to take a call. If you are not actually glad to take a call, it shows in your voice, no matter how big you fake the smile. The fix is to be in a condition where the smile is honest. Same lesson as everything else in this book — the inside leaks out.

What Kills a Phone Read

Just as fast as a voice can build trust, certain things can destroy it. Here are the ones I have heard kill calls again and again.

Picking up while still in another conversation. The customer hears you finishing a sentence with someone in the office before you turn to address them. They are now an interruption. The call started in a hole.

Answering with attitude. Maybe the morning has been rough. Maybe the last call was a bad one. Whatever it is, if your voice carries any edge — frustration, impatience, tired of this already — the customer hears it and reacts. They did not earn the edge. They got it anyway.

Reading the greeting from a script. Even a good greeting, if it is being read off a sheet rather than said, sounds wrong. The customer can hear the cadence of someone performing rather than speaking. Memorize the greeting until it is in your bones and you can say it like a normal sentence.

Hold without warning. Putting a caller on hold without first telling them, asking permission, and waiting for an answer is one of the fastest ways to lose them. "Can I put you on hold for just a moment?" pause "Of course" — that exchange takes three seconds and saves the call. Skipping it tells the customer their time is not respected.

Hold for too long. Even with permission, more than thirty seconds on hold is too long. If you need more time, come back, apologize briefly, and ask if it is okay to keep them holding or if you can call back. Customers who were left on long holds rate the experience worse than those who were told no, and they very rarely buy from a dealership that put them on hold for 2 minutes.

Hanging up first. Always let the customer hang up first. The click of you hanging up while they are still saying goodbye is a small thing, but it leaves a residue. A small, generous habit — waiting until the line goes dead on their end — gives the call a clean ending.

The Outbound Call

Most of what we have talked about is the inbound call—the customer calling you. The same principles apply to the outbound call, with one extra layer.

The customer who answered an outbound call did not ask to be called. They picked up, not knowing who was on the other end. Their guard is up by default. The ten-second window on an outbound call is even shorter and even harder, because you have to get past the initial "this is a sales call" reaction in the first sentence.

The move here is to be honest and brief. State who you are, where you are from, and why you are calling — in that order, in one short opening. "Hi, this is [Name] from [Dealership]. I'm following up on the inquiry you submitted last night about the [Vehicle]." That is twenty words. The customer knows immediately who you are, where you are from, and why you are calling. They can now decide whether to continue the conversation and do so in their own time.

What does not work is the slow build-up. "Hi, is this [Name]? How are you doing today? Great, great. Listen, the reason I'm calling is…" That entire windup makes the customer's ten-second read worse, because they spend the windup wondering when the pitch is coming. The pitch is the call—just get to it. Honesty about that is the move.

Closing the Loop

The phone is not a lesser version of the in-person sale. It is its own ten-second read, with its own signals, its own decisions, its own opportunities to win or lose. The salespeople who treat the phone as seriously as they treat the lot are the ones whose pipelines stay full. The salespeople who treat the phone as the thing they do with in-person customers are leaving deals on the table that they didn't even know existed.

Every call is a ten-second window. Every greeting is a first impression. Every voice tells the customer who you are before they have laid eyes on you. Answer the phone the way you would walk out the front door of the dealership — ready, present, in the kind of condition the customer will be glad they reached you.

"The Rule: The customer hears who you are in the first sentence of a phone call — sometimes in the first word. The voice carries everything the body would have. Answer every call like you are walking out to meet someone face to face."

CHAPTER 12

Building a First Impression That Works Every Time

B Y NOW, YOU SHOULD be looking at the ten-second window with different eyes.

You know what the customer is reading. You know the three decisions they are making. You know what your face, your pace, your energy, and your voice are telling them before you have opened your mouth. You know what to do when the read goes wrong. You know how it all works in the showroom and on the phone.

This chapter is the long game. Because none of what you have learned in this book is useful if it only shows up on your best days. The salesperson who can pull off a clean ten-second read when he is rested, focused, and in a good mood is not the salesperson I am trying to build with this book. The salesperson I am trying to build is the one who can pull off a clean ten-second read on a slow Tuesday in the middle of a bad month after a fight with his teenager that morning.

That salesperson is not performing. That salesperson is built.

Performance vs. Built

Performance is the version of yourself you put on when you walk out the door. It takes effort. It uses energy. It can be sustained for a few hours, but not for a full shift, and definitely not for a career. The salesperson running on performance burns out, and customers feel it before they even know what it is.

Built is different. Built is what happens when the things this book is about — calm energy, open expression, present attention, real curiosity — are no longer performances. They are who you are when you walk out the door, because you spent the time off the lot getting yourself into the kind of condition where those things show up on their own.

That difference is everything. The salesperson who is built does not have a ten-second window problem. He has a ten-second window habit. Every customer, every shift, every day, the read comes out clean because there is nothing to perform. The condition is already there.

So how do you become built? Not in ten seconds. Not in ten days. But in the daily, weekly, and monthly habits that determine what leaks out of you when a customer first lays eyes on you.

Sleep

I am going to start with the boring one because it matters most.

The sleep-deprived salesperson has a different face, voice, presence, and judgment than the salesperson who slept. Customers cannot tell you that you are tired. They can tell you that something seemed off. "Off" is usually the tired version of you, as seen by the customer's thin-slice instrument.

Sleep is not optional. It is not a luxury. It is not something you can catch up on Sunday. It is the floor on which the rest of your performance — your energy, your expression, your patience, your read on customers — either stands or collapses. The salespeople with the longest careers are not the ones who work the longest hours. They are the ones who treat their sleep like a job requirement.

Seven hours minimum. Eight is better. Most of the salespeople reading this book are not getting either, and most of them think they are doing fine. They are not doing fine. They are doing fine compared to the worst version of themselves, who got even less sleep. The actual ceiling on their performance is much higher than what they are seeing.

If you take one habit out of this chapter, take this one. Sleep. Every night. Like the job depends on it. Because it does.

What You Put in Your Body

I am not your nutritionist. But I will tell you what I have watched for thirty-five years on car lots.

The salesperson who runs on convenience-store food and energy drinks has a different ten-second presence than the salesperson who eats something that resembles food. The crash from a high-sugar diet shows up in the face, the eyes, the pace, and the patience around three in the afternoon — exactly when many customers walk in. The salesperson who is crashing is going to fail the ten-second read with the four o'clock customer, no matter how much he knows about this stuff.

You do not have to eat perfectly. You have to eat well enough so the crash doesn't happen on your shift. Protein in the morning. Water throughout the day. Something with actual vegetables in it somewhere. The basics. Nobody is asking you to become a health magazine. They are asking you not to run on fumes at the exact moment a customer is reading you.

Movement

Same principle. The salesperson who is moving his body during the week — walking, lifting, biking, anything — carries a different presence onto the lot than the salesperson who is sitting all the time.

This is not about how you look. This is about what is happening inside you. A body that moves regularly is a body that handles stress better, sleeps better, and carries less tension into a stranger's view. You can iron your shirt all you want. If your body underneath it is locked up from sitting for fifteen hours a day, the customer is going to read the tension, even if they cannot name what they are reading.

Twenty minutes a day. Three or four days a week. Move. Walk the lot if that is what you have. The salesperson who is moving carries a different ten-second window than the one who is not, and customers will read the difference whether they know it or not.

Handle Your Stuff

We talked about this in Chapter 4, but it bears repeating.

Whatever you are carrying — the strained marriage, the kid who is struggling, the tight money, the anger you have toward the manager, the regret you have about a deal that fell through last week — if you have not done any work on it, it shows. The customer cannot tell you what it is. But they can feel that you are not all the way there with them, and they react to that by not being all the way there with you.

Handling your stuff does not mean solving it. Some of what you are carrying is not solvable. Handling it means doing the work of looking at it, naming it, getting whatever help you need with it — a conversation, a counselor, a phone call to someone who knows you — so that it is not just rotting inside you while you are trying to do your job.

The salespeople who consistently have great ten-second windows are the salespeople who have done some work on themselves outside the lot. They are not necessarily happy. They are not necessarily relaxed. But they are not at war with what they are carrying, and that absence of internal war shows up as the calm the customer feels.

Reset Habits Between Customers

Here is a small one that pays off enormously. Between every customer interaction — not every hour, every customer — do a reset.

Thirty seconds. Go to a window. Stand at the side of the building. Get a glass of water. Whatever lets you step out of the conversation that just ended and put it down before the next one starts.

Breathe. Drop your shoulders. Unclench your jaw. Settle your eyes. Look at something in the middle distance. Let what just happened be done.

Then walk back into the floor as if it is the first customer of the day. Because for the customer who just pulled in, it is.

Salespeople who do not do this are draining the energy of customer one into customer two, then into customer three, and then into the rest of the shift. By the eighth customer, the energy has accumulated into something heavy that the eighth customer reads in two seconds. Reset—every time. Customers should not pay for the customer who came before them.

Self-Awareness

All of the above is wasted if you cannot see yourself.

The salespeople with the most consistent ten-second reads are the salespeople who can check in with themselves at any moment and know what they are bringing into the next interaction. "Am I rushed? Am I tense? Am I distracted? Am I bringing the last customer in with me?" The check-in is not a constant analysis. It is a quick, honest look in the mirror that you do as a habit, like an athlete checking his form between reps.

Awareness is most of the battle. You cannot adjust what you cannot see. The salesperson who knows he is rushed can do something about it. The salesperson who is rushed and does not know it cannot.

Spend some time off the lot building the habit of noticing your own state. It will pay off in front of every customer for the rest of your career.

And Then — Sometimes None of It Matters

Here is the part I want you to hear, because if I do not say it, you might walk out of this book thinking the work is purely on your end.

Sometimes you do everything right, and the read still goes bad. Not because you missed a signal. Not because you sent a wrong one. Because of something that has nothing to do with you, and could not have been controlled by anything you did.

Like this.

FROM THE FLOOR

I had a colleague who couldn't get any traction with a woman at the used-car lot. She kept saying she was just looking. He couldn't figure out what was off—he'd done everything right as far as he could tell. He came and got me.

I went out, introduced myself, and asked how I could help her.

She said: "God, thank you. I really want to buy this car. But that other guy looks exactly like my ex-husband, and I cannot stand the sight of him."

Nothing to do with the car. Nothing to do with the approach. She knew exactly what she wanted — she just needed a different person in front of her before she would let the conversation happen. We tested the vehicle, worked out fair numbers, and she drove home happy.

Don't take "I'm just looking" personally. Don't take it as a verdict. Take it as information — something needs to be adjusted. Sometimes that's your approach. Sometimes it's giving more space. And occasionally it's a different person entirely. All of those are workable. None of them is the end of the deal.

That salesperson did nothing wrong. He could have read every chapter of this book and still failed that ten-second read, because the read was about something he could not change. His face. The way he walked. Something. The customer's reaction was not to him as a salesperson — it was to a memory she could not separate from his face.

Most of the time, when a first impression fails, you can trace it back to something you did. Most of the time. But not every time. And the salespeople who are built right do not turn every failure into a referendum on themselves. They look at it, ask whether there was something to learn, and if the answer is no—if it was just one of those situations where the customer brought in something you couldn't see—they let it go and move on to the next one.

Building a first impression that works every time does not mean it succeeds every time. It means a first impression that comes from a place where you have done the work. From a built version of yourself rather than a performed one. Some of those will still fail — because some failures are not yours — but the ones that do not will multiply, and the ones that do fail will not stick to you the way they stick to a salesperson winging it.

That is the long game. That is what this whole book has been pointing toward. Not a trick. Not a script. A built version of yourself who walks out the door every day in a condition where the ten-second window is a strength, not a hazard.

Build it. One habit at a time. One shift at a time. One reset between customers at a time. The salesperson you become over a year of that work is the salesperson the customer reads in ten seconds and decides, "Yes — I can talk to this person."

"The Rule: A first impression that works every time is not a performance — it is a condition. Build the condition off the lot, and the ten seconds will take care of themselves."

Chapter 13

The Ten-Second Checklist

THIS CHAPTER IS SHORTER than the others. On purpose.

Everything in this book up to now has been the explanation. This chapter is the distillation. Two checklists — one for the start of your shift, one for right before you walk out to meet a customer. Both short. Both direct. Both are designed to be used, not admired.

Read this chapter once for understanding. Then come back to it before every shift, and before every customer, until the items on the checklist are running in your head, whether you are looking at the page or not. That is when the work this book is about becomes a habit instead of an effort.

The Pre-Shift Checklist

Before you walk into the building today, run this list. Five minutes. Whatever you cannot fix in those five minutes is information about what to work on for tomorrow.

• Did I sleep enough? If the answer is no, today will require more deliberate awareness than usual. Plan for it.

• Did I eat? Something with protein. Not just coffee. The crash is real, and customers will pay for it later if I skip this now.

• Are my clothes clean and pressed? Mirror check. Not the kind mirror — the customer mirror. Would a stranger looking at me think this person takes the job seriously?

- Are my shoes acceptable? Wiped down at a minimum, and replaced if beyond wiping down.

- Hair, grooming, breath. Combed, trimmed, fresh. Mints in the pocket.

- Is there anything I am carrying today that I have not handled? The argument from this morning. The overdue bill. The phone call I have been putting off. If something is going to leak out of me, it is one of those. Either handle it now or acknowledge it so it does not run me from underneath.

- What is my energy honestly like right now? Not what I want it to be. What is it? Calm? Tense? Rushed? Distracted? Knowing the honest answer is the first step to managing it.

- Am I ready to be present with whoever walks in first today? If not, what do I need—five more minutes, a glass of water, a quick walk—before I am ready?

The Pre-Approach Checklist

Before you walk out the door or across the showroom to meet a customer who just arrived. Ten seconds. Run this in your head every time.

- Unclench my jaw.

- Drop my shoulders.

- Soften my eyes.

- Settle my pace. Calm walk. Not a sprint. Not a drag. The pace of someone with time for this.

- Put the last customer down. Whatever just happened with the last person is done. This person is not paying for it.

- Notice everyone. Not just the buyer. Spouse, kids, friend, parent. Plan to acknowledge each of them.

- Hold the right question. "What does this person need from me right now?" Not "is this a buyer?" Not "how do I move this toward a close?" Just that one question. Curious. Open. Real.

- Plan my first sentence. Short. Hospitable. No question that requires them to commit to anything. "Hey, welcome in. Take your time — just let me know if you have a question." Or some version of that, in your own voice.

Between Customers

And one more, the smallest of all. Between every customer interaction, run this.

- Did I close that one out clean? Whether the customer bought or left, did I end it well?
- What energy am I carrying from that interaction? Is any of it going to leak into the next one if I do not put it down?
- Thirty seconds. Water. Window. Breath. Reset.
- Walk back onto the floor as if it were the first customer of the day.

Why This Works

Checklists feel small. They are not. The pilots who have flown for forty years and never had a serious incident are the ones who still run the checklist before every flight. Not because they do not know the airplane. Because checklists are how you keep the small things from ruining everything else.

The ten-second window is exactly that kind of thing. It is small. It is fast. It is easy to skip past without thinking about it. And it is the thing that decides, more than anything else, how the next forty-five minutes will go.

Use the checklists. Every shift. Every customer. Until they are no longer checklists — just the way you operate.

That is when this book stops being something you read and starts being how you work.

"The Rule: Checklists are not for people who do not know what they are doing — they are for people who refuse to forget what they know. Run yours before every shift and every customer, until the list is just who you are."

CONCLUSION

Ten seconds.

That is what this whole book has been about. The window that opens the second a customer becomes aware of you and closes about the time you finish your first sentence. The window in which everything that will matter over the next forty-five minutes is decided.

Most salespeople have no idea this window exists. They think the work starts when the conversation starts. They think the first impression is the handshake. They walk out to meet customers without understanding what has already happened in the customer's head before they get there, and they spend the rest of the interaction trying to overcome an impression they did not even know they made.

You are not going to be one of those salespeople anymore.

You know what the customer is reading—the appearance, the pace, the face, the energy, the eyes. You know what the customer is deciding. Safe or not safe. Respectful or not. Honest or not. You know what to do when the read goes wrong and which habits to build so that it goes right more often than it goes wrong. You know how the rules change in the showroom and on the phone. You know which signals you can control and which you cannot. You know that some of the work is in the ten seconds, and most of it is everywhere else.

That knowledge alone is going to change how you walk out the door tomorrow. You will notice things you did not notice before. You are going to slow down where you used to rush. You will read customers more accurately.

You are going to make different choices in the small moments that used to feel like nothing.

And here is what will happen over time. The customers who used to say "just looking" and walk away are going to stay a little longer. The conversations that used to feel like they were uphill from the start are going to feel easier. The deals that used to feel like they'd never close are going to close. Not because you became a more aggressive salesperson. Because you became one who can pass the test the customer is running in the first ten seconds.

That is the whole game. The customer who has decided you are safe, respectful, and honest is the customer who will tell you what they need. They will let you guide them. They will buy from you. They will come back. They will refer their friends. None of that happens with the customer whose ten-second read came out wrong.

Make the ten seconds work for you. Not as a trick. Not as a performance. As a habit. It's the natural product of who you are when you walk onto the lot, because you put in the work to be that version of yourself before you stepped out the door.

Ten seconds is all you get. Now you know what to do with them.

Get out there.

"The Rule: Everything that matters in the first impression happens in ten seconds — and almost none of the work to win those ten seconds happens inside them. Build the salesperson off the lot. The window will take care of itself."

Tips for the Sales Manager

If you are a sales manager reading this book, the ten-second rule applies to you twice.

It applies to the salespeople you are training, because they have to be able to win the read on the lot. And it applies to the floor as a whole, because the room they work in is itself sending a ten-second message to every customer who walks through the door. The salesperson can do everything right in the field and still lose to a showroom that failed the read before anyone got to the customer.

Here is what to focus on if you want your team to consistently win the ten-second window.

Watch the Approach, Not the Pitch

Most sales coaching happens in the wrong part of the conversation. Managers ride along on the call, listen in on the negotiation, and review the deal afterward. All of that is downstream. The deal was usually decided in the first ten seconds, long before the part that most managers pay attention to.

Spend more time watching the approach. Stand at the window. Watch your team walk out to meet customers. Watch the pace, the posture, the face. Watch how they greet. Watch whether they acknowledge everyone at the party or just the driver. The information you get from five minutes of watching approaches is worth more than an hour of reviewing closed deals.

And then talk to them about what you saw. Not in a write-up. Not in a formal review. In a thirty-second conversation as they come back inside. "I noticed you walked out fast — you doing okay?" That kind of question opens up the conversation about what is actually happening at the front of the funnel.

Fix the Room

The showroom passes or fails the ten-second test as a group. That is your job to manage, not theirs.

Things you are on the hook for fixing. Whether someone is positioned to quickly greet walk-ins. Whether the receptionist is trained on what a good first greeting sounds like. Whether the floor is organized and clean. Whether the energy of the room reads as a working business or as a graveyard. Whether the salespeople who are between customers know how to look engaged and not like they are wishing the day was over.

Walk into your own showroom from outside, the way a customer would, once a week. Not at opening. In the middle of a normal shift. Notice what you notice in the first ten seconds. If anything is off, fix it. The room is talking to every customer who walks in, and you are the one with the authority to shape what it says.

Coach the New Ones on Energy Before Technique

New salespeople are usually taught the script first. The greeting line. The walk-around. The objection handlers. All of which are useful eventually, and all of which are wasted if the new salesperson cannot pass the ten-second read.

The smarter sequence is energy first, technique second. Get them to a place where they can walk out onto the lot calm, present, and human — even when they are nervous, which they will be. The technique becomes vastly more effective on top of a good ten-second window. The technique is almost useless on top of a bad one.

Spend some of your training time on the unglamorous stuff. The pre-shift checklist. The reset between customers. The way to look up when the door opens. The default face. The pace of the walk. New salespeople do not think those things are real. The veterans on your floor know they are everything.

Catch the Pattern Early

Salespeople who consistently lose customers in the first thirty seconds usually have one or two specific things they do wrong on the approach. The same things. Every time. They cannot see it because it is invisible to them — it is their default. But it is visible to you from across the lot.

Pay attention to which of your salespeople have the highest "just looking" rate. The ones whose customers leave fastest. The ones whose conversations end before they begin. That is rarely a closing problem. It is almost always a ten-second window problem.

Watch those salespeople specifically. Identify the pattern. Then have the conversation. Not in front of others. Not as a criticism. As an observation. "I noticed you do this when you walk out — I wonder if customers are reading it as that. Want to try a different version for a few days and see what happens?" Salespeople are generally grateful when someone finally points out the thing they could not see for themselves. They have been losing customers for a reason they did not know existed.

Protect the Reset

Salespeople need to be able to reset between customers. Thirty seconds at a window. A glass of water. A breath. If your culture punishes this — if salespeople feel they have to be back on the floor instantly, or if taking thirty seconds looks like slacking — you are going to have a team that drags every bad interaction into the next one.

Make the reset acceptable. Make it normal. Let your team see you doing it. The result is a floor where every customer gets the version of the salesperson they deserve, not the one still carrying the previous customer's frustration.

Be the Example

Last one. The ten-second window applies to you as a manager, too. The way you walk through the showroom. The way you talk to your team. The way you greet customers when you have to step in. All of it is being watched by both the team and any customers in earshot.

A manager who walks through the showroom, rushed, frustrated, or distracted, is teaching the team that this is how it is done here. A manager who walks through calmly, attentively, and steadily is teaching them the same thing. You are demonstrating the ten-second rule whether you mean to or not. Make sure what you are demonstrating is what you want them to learn.

The team will be as good at the ten-second window as their manager is. That is just how it works. Set the standard with your own behavior, and the standard becomes the floor for theirs.

APPENDIX

The Rules

Every chapter in this book ended with The Rule—the single most important principle of that chapter, stated plainly. They are collected here for easy reference. Read them. Write them down. Put them somewhere you will see them before your next shift.

"The Rule: The customer has already started forming an impression before you open your mouth. Your job is to make sure that impression works in your favor, not against you."

— Introduction

"The Rule: Customers form a complete, lasting impression of you in the first ten seconds — not because they choose to, but because their brain is built to. Your job is to know what they are reading and make sure it lands in your favor."

— Chapter 1

"The Rule: The customer's impression of you started forming before you said a word — and before you knew they were watching. Manage the signals you send when no one is looking, because someone always is."

— Chapter 2

"The Rule: How you look is the first thing the customer reads, and they read it in less than a second. Showing up sharp does not win the

sale by itself — but showing up sloppy can lose it before you say a word.”

— Chapter 3

“The Rule: Customers read your energy before they read your words — and your energy is set hours before you walk onto the lot. Take care of what you carry in, because every customer is going to feel it.”

— Chapter 4

“The Rule: Your face is talking before your mouth is, and your default face is the one customers read first. Make sure what it is saying is something you would actually want said.”

— Chapter 5

“The Rule: The customer can tell the difference between a salesperson who wants to help and one who wants to sell — from across the lot, before anyone speaks. Walk out with the right question in your head and the right one will show on your face.”

— Chapter 6

“The Rule: In the first ten seconds, the customer is not deciding whether to buy a car. They are deciding whether you are safe, respectful, and honest. Win those three, and the rest of the conversation has a chance. Lose any one of them and the rest is just stalling.”

— Chapter 7

“The Rule: When the first impression goes wrong, the customer’s body will tell you long before their mouth does. Read the signals, stop talking, and admit to yourself what happened — because you cannot fix what you refuse to see.”

— Chapter 8

“The Rule: A bad first impression can be reset — but only by dropping the original plan, acknowledging something real in the moment, and putting the customer’s comfort ahead of your agenda. The salesperson who is willing to lose the deal to do that is the salesperson who recovers the most of them.”

— Chapter 9

"The Rule: The walk-in customer reads the whole room in ten seconds, not just the salesperson. If you cannot fix the room, fix your corner of it — and be the head that turns when the door opens."

— Chapter 10

"The Rule: The customer hears who you are in the first sentence of a phone call — sometimes in the first word. The voice carries everything the body would have. Answer every call like you are walking out to meet someone face to face."

— Chapter 11

"The Rule: A first impression that works every time is not a performance — it is a condition. Build the condition off the lot, and the ten seconds will take care of themselves."

— Chapter 12

"The Rule: Checklists are not for people who do not know what they are doing — they are for people who refuse to forget what they know. Run yours before every shift and every customer, until the list is just who you are."

— Chapter 13

Also Available

The flagship work and the full Car Sales Survival Guide Series:

The Complete Car Sales Survival Guide

The No-BS Playbook for New Automotive Salespeople

Book 1 — The Meet and Greet Playbook

How to Make Powerful First Impressions with Customers, Clients, and Guests

Book 2 — The First 60 Seconds in Car Sales

A Proven Meet and Greet System to Build Trust and Start More Conversations

Book 3 — How to Handle "I'm Just Looking" in Car Sales

A Simple System to Turn Brush-Offs into Productive Conversations

Book 4 — Body Language in Car Sales

How Posture, Eye Contact, and Presence Build Customer Trust

Book 5 — Greeting Customers on the Lot

How to Approach Buyers Without Pressure

Book 6 — The Ten-Second Rule in Car Sales

Why First Impressions Determine Whether Customers Stay or Leave

Book 7 — The Car Sales Conversation Starter Guide

How to Begin Natural Conversations That Lead to Sales

Book 8 — Car Sales Confidence for New Salespeople

How to Approach Customers Without Fear or Hesitation

Book 9 — Common Car Sales Greeting Mistakes

What Drives Customers Away in the First Minute

Book 10 — The First Five Minutes With a Car Buyer

How to Transition from Greeting to Conversation and Move Toward the Sale

Available wherever books are sold.

www.bedrockheritagepublishing.com

WORK WITH BRUCE

If you're interested in one-on-one coaching, sales team training, or dealership consulting, Bruce works with individuals and organizations through Life Guidance Consulting.

For inquiries:

www.lifeguidanceconsulting.com

bruce@lifeguidanceconsulting.com

For publishing inquiries or bulk orders:

www.bedrockheritagepublishing.com

info@bedrockheritagepublishing.com

About the Author

Bruce Huddleston spent thirty-five years in the automotive industry, working every level of the business from showroom floor salesperson to finance manager, sales manager, used car manager, and general manager. His career included new-car franchise dealerships, independent used-car operations, and a decade in buy-here, pay-here — giving him a breadth of experience that few in the industry can match.

He began as a high school dropout who needed a job and ended up discovering a profession. He ended as a veteran who had trained hundreds of salespeople, managed multiple departments, and built a reputation for straight talk in an industry that doesn't always reward it.

Since retiring, Bruce has opened a life coaching practice, assists his wife with her mental health therapy practice, and operates Bedrock Heritage Publishing, a division of Life Guidance Consulting LLC, where he writes practical guides for sales professionals across multiple industries.

The Complete Car Sales Survival Guide is his flagship work. The Car Sales Survival Guide Series — a collection of focused training guides on specific sales skills — is built on the same foundation of real experience, honest insight, and zero tolerance for the kind of nonsense that gives sales a bad name.

He lives in Tyler, Texas.

A Quick Favor

If The Ten Second Rule in Car Sales helped you — if it changed how you walk onto a lot, how you read a customer, or how you think about what your body is saying before you open your mouth — I'd be grateful if you'd take two minutes to leave a review wherever you bought it.

Reviews matter more than most people realize. They help other salespeople find books that can actually make a difference in their work. And honest feedback helps me keep writing things worth reading.

You can simply scan the QR code below.

https://www.amazon.com/review/create-review/?asin=1972179144

www.bedrockheritagepublishing.com